JAPAN
is my country

In this book 26 people from all over Japan
tell you what their life is like – life in the city,
life on the coast and life in the countryside.

Bernice and Cliff Moon

Marshall Cavendish
New York · London · Sydney · Toronto

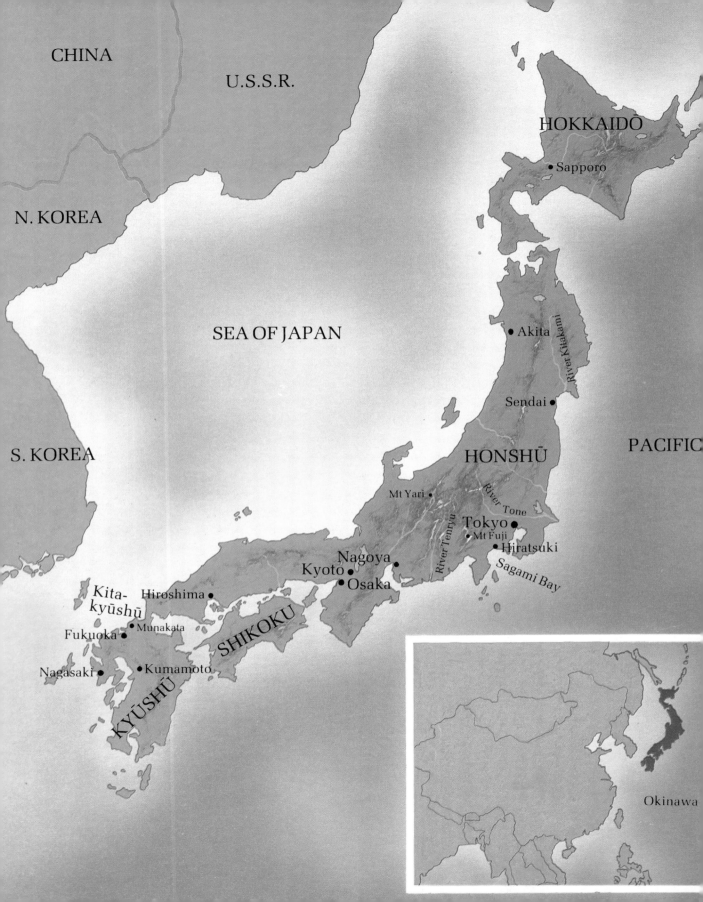

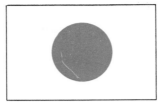

Stands for a red sun. Japan is known as the "Land of the Rising Sun".

National Anthem
"The Peaceful Reign"

Crane

Cherry Tree

Cherry Blossom

JAPAN
GLOSSARY:

Chopsticks: Two small sticks used for eating

Diet: Japanese national parliament

Geology: The study of rocks and rock formations

Imperial Palace: Emperor's palace

Kimono: Loose robe worn by both men and women in Japan

Kyushu: Most southerly of the main islands of Japan

Miming: Telling a story by movement

Olympic Games: World athletics championships held every four years

Paddy: Flooded field in which rice is grown

Temple: Place of worship

Tempura: Japanese fried seafood dish

Based on original text and photographs by Chris Fairclough

Cover photograph: Toshogu Shrine in Nikko
H. Wölk – Zefa

Reference Edition published 1986
My Country Series – Volume 9

© Marshall Cavendish Limited MCMLXXXVI
© Wayland (Publishers) Limited MCMLXXXIV

Published by Marshall Cavendish Corporation
147 West Merrick Road
Freeport
Long Island
N.Y. 11520

Library of Congress Cataloging in Publication Data

Main entry under title:

My Country Series

Volumes in the British Edition are published under their respective analytical titles, e.g., Greece – My Country Series

Includes indexes

Summary: A series of books including first person accounts of various ways of life in twenty different countries.

1. Geography – Juvenile Literature – collected works. (1. Geography)
1. Marshall Cavendish Corporation

G133, C68, 1985 949, 5'07 85-22397

ISBN 0-86307-476-6 (Lib-Bdg.: Set)
ISBN 0-86307-471-5 (This Volume)

Printed in Italy by G. Canale & C.S.p.A., Turin

CONTENTS

My name is Yoshie and I am a student.

I am 12 years old and I go to school
in the city of Munakata on the island of Kyūshū.
Japan is made up of four main islands
and over 3,000 smaller islands.

I love music and
I practice on the piano
every day after school.
Then I do my homework and
look after my sister
until my mother and father
come home from work.

Our school year starts in April when the days are warm.
That is when we go on lots of trips to the hills and parks.
Summer vacation is in July and August when it's hot,
so many families go to the seaside or into the mountains.
We go back to school in September and that is when
we have our sports day.
We have piggyback fights, races, relays and dancing.
School closes again at the end of December and
we all look forward to the New Year.
The winter term is very short and in the middle of March
we have our spring vacation.

My teacher is called Harada and she is very kind.
I would like to be a teacher when I grow up.

I am Shiun and I make dolls.

Dolls have been made in Japan for many years.
I am 70 years old and I have been making them for 50 years.

I make all the different parts of the dolls' bodies.
Then I paint them very carefully.

Let me tell you how I make a doll.
First I carve wooden molds for all the parts of the body.
Then I make a mixture of starch and sawdust.
This is soft like clay and I press it into the molds.
When the mixture is set hard I take the parts out of the molds
and paint them all with three layers of paint.
Then I put in the eyes and paint on the makeup.
I have to be very careful when I do this.
Next I draw the face, color the cheeks and fit the hair,
which is real human hair.
I then fit the head, legs and arms onto the body and
lastly I dress the doll in a robe called a kimono.

These dolls are finished.
You can see how carefully
I had to paint their faces.
Their kimonos are just like
the real ones that Japanese
women sometimes wear.

I am Masako and I'm a tourist guide.

I work for the biggest sight-seeing company in Tokyo.
People come to Tokyo from all over Japan and
from all over the world.
My job is to show them around.
I can only speak Japanese so I am a guide for Japanese visitors.
I either take them by bus on a short tour of our capital city
for four hours, or on a longer tour for eleven hours.
Lots of schoolchildren come on our tours in spring and fall.
I like taking them to Mount Fuji which is near Tokyo.
I like to sing to my passengers as we go along and
I'm always trying to think of new songs they will enjoy.

Here you can see me
having my photograph taken
with one of my groups.
We are in front of
the Nijubashi Bridge which
is the main entrance
to the Imperial Palace
in Tokyo.

I usually walk in front
of the tourists.
I hold up a flag so
they won't get lost
when we're in a crowd.

My name is Masao. I'm a traffic policeman

Ten years ago my father was killed in a road accident.
I was so upset that I joined the "white bikers"
who patrol central Tokyo to make sure that people
obey all the traffic laws.

Here I am on patrol
on my white bike
in the center of Tokyo.
I keep my eyes open for
youngsters on motorcycles.
Some of them ride around
at high speed and
cause terrible accidents.

The roads are very busy in the center of Tokyo.
There are more accidents here than in any other Japanese city.
We get about 30,000 accidents a year in Tokyo and
most of them are caused by speeding.

Our white bikes are very heavy and very powerful.
Someettimes we have to go fast to catch cars or motorbikes
which are breaking the speed limit, but
we are well trained and I keep myself fit by doing judo.
I usually patrol for about five hours a day but
it can be longer when there are traffic problems.

My name is Fuku.
I am a teacher.

You may think that I'm a rather unusual teacher because I teach people how to arrange flowers, eat cake and drink tea!
These girls are learning how to mix tea properly in a bowl.

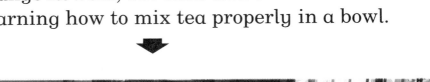

For many years we Japanese have believed that tea
should be made and drunk in a special way.
It takes several months to learn how to eat the cakes
which we serve with the tea, and
it takes a year to learn how to drink tea in the correct way.

I also teach people
how to arrange flowers.
I show my pupils how to
place the flowers so that
they will look as attractive
as possible.
I teach fifteen pupils
of all ages.

To the Japanese, tea making
and flower arranging are
arts which help to bring more
beauty into the world.

I am Mitsunaga. I'm a ferry captain.

There are people living on
440 of the small islands
that surround Japan.
I live on Okinawa which is at
the southern end of all these
islands.
My wooden house has
a tiled roof.
Houses in Okinawa have been
built like this for hundreds
of years.

18

I am the captain of this large ferry boat, the *Sunshine Okinawa*.
We carry passengers between Tokyo and Okinawa.

It takes over two days to sail the 1,024 miles (1,648 km)
between Okinawa and Tokyo.
My ferry is usually full of vacationers
who love to visit the beautiful island of Okinawa.
I also take lots of business people to and from Tokyo.

I am always up at six o'clock in the morning and
the first thing I do is check the weather.
When the sea is calm I can relax because I know
that my passengers will have a good trip.
But if the sea gets rough or
if sailing is difficult because of fog or rain,
then I have to work hard all the way.

I am Kazutaro and I'm a train driver.

Have you ever heard of the Japanese "bullet" trains?
They are called that because they travel so fast.
The first bullet train ran from Tokyo to Osaka in 1964.
It was called *Hikari 2* and I was the driver.

Here is my bullet train.
I check the engine
every day.
It is very different from the
steam trains that I used to
drive years ago.

Bullet trains are controlled by computer.
They each have 15 cars and can travel at
more than 130 m.p.h. (210 km/h).
Sometimes there are as many as 280 bullet trains running
each day, and there are more than 1,000 bullet train drivers.

Each train has one or two drivers, as well as an inspector and
three conductors.
I usually drive between Tokyo and Osaka three times in six days
and then I have a few days off.

The trains are run by
electricity and they are
very safe.
We haven't had a bad
accident since the service
started in 1964.

I am Nachisa.
I'm an automobile worker.

I expect you've heard of Datsun automobiles.
I work for the Nissan car company which makes Datsuns.
We sell our cars all over the world.
The factory where I work is outside Tokyo.

Here I am working
on the inside of my
favorite Datsun automobile,
a sports car that
we call the Fairlady Z.

Japanese car firms were among the first to use robots.
Robots work quickly and they do not make mistakes.
But we still need people to work in automobile factories.
I work on the inside of the cars, putting in instrument panels.
A car can look wonderful from the outside but
the inside has to be comfortable enough for long journeys.
I try to treat each car as though it were my own.

I went to work for Nissan because they make my favorite
car, the Datsun 280ZK, also known as the Fairlady Z.
It has six cylinders and is cheaper many than other sports cars.

These Datsun cars are waiting at the docks
to be taken by ship to Europe.

My name is Masae and I'm a rice farmer.

I live in the center of Honshū, the main island of Japan. There are high mountains all around my farm.

This is the Nagano district where I live and work. It is very cold in the mountains in winter but in summer it is cool and fresh. My son has gone to work in Tokyo and my husband is a builder so I run the farm on my own.

Every morning at 8 o'clock I start work in the rice fields.
Rice plants are really marsh plants so they always need
to be covered with plenty of water.
A rice field is called a *paddy* and the first thing I do
each morning is to check the water level in the paddies.
Rice farmers are always busiest at planting time in May,
at weeding time in June and July, and at harvest time
in the fall.

It is weeding time.
This job always makes
my back ache.
When winter comes there
is nothing to do
in the paddies so
I stay indoors and knit
clothes and toys
for my family.

I am Yasuhiro and I'm a judo champion.

I have been judo champion of Japan several times and world champion twice.
I would like to win a medal at the Olympic Games.

I practice for hours to try and get all the different judo holds exactly right.
When I'm not practicing I work as a researcher at Tokai University in Tokyo.

To be really good at judo you have to train your mind
as well as your body.

I was born at Kumamoto on the island of Kyūshū and,
by the time I started school, I was big for my age.
I often got into fights in the playground and
I used to hurt other children without meaning to.
So when I was 9 years old my mother sent me
to a judo school where I could let off steam.
Soon I became the best in my age group in the whole of Japan,
and people began to call me the "Monster Child!"

I'm Hiroshi and I own a restaurant.

My restaurant is in central Tokyo.
It is very small and can seat only 16 customers.
My mother and father help me with the cooking.
I take one day off a week, and then I like to go swimming.

Here I am with
my mother outside my
little restaurant.
My dream is to own
a bigger restaurant
in a better part
of Tokyo.

We cook a delicious Japanese dish called *tempura*.
It is made from all kinds of seafood and vegetables
which are coated in a flour mixture and then fried.
It took me 6 years to learn how to cook tempura properly.
I always use fresh fish which I get from
the market every morning.
I buy prawns, eels, squid and various kinds of fish.
I spend all morning cooking so that
I am ready for my first customers who arrive at 11 a.m.
We get about 60 customers a day and
whole families often come here for a meal.

This is what *tempura* looks like, with fried fish and vegetables
and lots of little dishes of food.

I am Tsusho.
I'm a priest.

I am a priest at the Buddhist temple in Tokyo.
Buddhism is one of the great religions of the world.
It began in India many years ago and then it spread to the East.
The religion was founded by a man we call the Buddha.
He tried to teach people how to live together peacefully.
His teachings say that people often make bad mistakes
because they are two worried about money and power.

I try to help people by teaching the ways of Buddha.
I also help people who have run away from home or
who have problems in their families.
I have even been godfather to an abandoned baby.

30

These are the gardens
of the Buddhist
temple in Tokyo.

I pray like this in
the temple every day.
Young priests are trained
by shutting themselves in
the temple for 100 days.
They sleep for only 3 hours
a day and they have only
watery rice to eat.

31

I am Tsuneko.
I'm a teacher.

I live with my husband and two sons at Fukuoka
on Kyūshū in southern Japan.
I teach English at a school for 12- to 15-year-olds.

I spend a lot of time
marking my pupils' work
and getting lessons ready
for the next day.
At the end of term
there are exams to mark
and reports to write.

Japanese children go to elementary school from the age of 6 to 12, middle school from 12 to 15, and high school from 16 to 18. All children have to go to elementary and middle school. I decided to study English because I wanted to travel.

Japanese people find English a difficult language to learn. It is very hard for them to learn how to pronounce English words. English is very different from Japanese and only a few of my pupils are really good at it.

I'm Hajime.
I sell cameras.

You may have heard of a Japanese camera called a Pentax.
I work at the Pentax factory just outside Tokyo.
It's my job to sell our cameras to other countries.

This is the modern factory where Pentax cameras are made.

All these workers are making Pentax cameras.

In Japan everyone has a camera, and I mean *everyone,*
not just one camera per family!
Many of our new cameras are fully automatic.
This means that you don't have to be an expert photographer
to take really good pictures.
Every camera company is trying to make light, easy-to-use,
low-priced cameras these days because that's what people want.

I have worked in some of our offices abroad and was in
West Germany for 7 years.
It is a beautiful country and I should love to go back there.

My name is Kimiko and I am a housewife.

I am 32 years old and I live in Tokyo with my husband, my three little girls, my parents and my grandmother.

We are a big family and at meal times there are eight of us around the table.

We all live in a two-story house
which was built more than 100 years ago.
We have three Japanese-style rooms, two Western-style rooms
and a kitchen.
The house is quite big but we don't have much storage space.

Cooking is quite difficult because everyone in the family likes
to eat different things.
My daughters like to eat hamburgers, curry and soup.
On the other hand my husband likes *tempura* and meat,
while my parents would rather have Japanese stew.
Shopping isn't easy either because the food I buy
doesn't seem to be as good as it used to be.
I try to keep my girls fit by taking them for swimming lessons
and I have joined a volleyball club to keep myself fit.

Every day I go to
the supermarket.
I try to choose
the freshest food.

I am Shigeru and I'm a reporter.

I work as a reporter for the *Hokkaidō Times,*
the local paper for Hokkaidō Island,
which is the most northerly island of Japan.
Hokkaidō is a beautiful, unspoiled place but it's very cold
in winter.

I studied journalism at
Tokyo University before
I became a reporter.
Today I am getting
a story ready for
the next edition of the
Hokkaidō Times.

I write stories about sporting events such as this speedboat race.

In my first years as a reporter I found the work very hard and
the hours very long.
But when readers wrote in to say how good they thought my
stories were, I realized I was doing a useful job.
I still work long hours most days and get very tired but
I don't mind as long as people enjoy reading what I write.
The Japanese are great readers and altogether we have
126 newspapers in Japan.

I am Kimiko and I run a kimono store.

The Japanese have always liked wearing kimonos.
A kimono is a loose garment with very wide sleeves
and it is tied around the waist with a wide sash.
Kimonos are comfortable to wear because they are so loose.
Some of the kimonos I sell in my store are very expensive
and they can cost as much as $3,000.
My store is in Sendai on the island of Kyūshū.
Our family has been running a kimono store
for more than 100 years.

If you came to my store to buy a kimono,
I would first show you lots of different rolls of cloth
and you would choose the one you liked best.
Then one of our tailors would make your kimono.

Kimonos are still worn
on Japanese festival days.

This woman is trying on
her new kimono.
It is very beautiful but
it is expensive.

I am Shigehito.
I'm a forester.

I live in a village called Tatsuyama which is
in the mountains just above the River Tenryu.
It is a small village with about 2,000 people.
Most of these people are either forestry workers or tea growers.

Today I am felling trees
in the forest.
Most of the trees
are cedars or cypresses.

I began by working in the forestry office but
two years ago I was asked if I would be in charge
of the cutting and planting of trees.
We usually work high in the mountains above the village and
we cannot get there by road so we have to walk.
It can be tough climbing up and down mountains all day!
We have to look after our young trees very carefully
so that one day that will produce good timber.
Most of my day is spent clearing away the grass and plants
which grow around the trees.
I also have to trim off the branches when the trees are felled.

I look forward to my cup of tea and Japanese stew
when we stop work at lunch time.
Today we're lucky because we can travel to work in a van.

My name is Sohshin and I'm a teacher.

I teach children and adults how to paint Japanese letters.
We have had this lovely writing for thousands of years and
we don't want our people to forget how it's done.
I also edit a magazine about Japanese writing.

My own pictures of
really big letters are
difficult to paint.
I have to keep my brush
moving all the time and
I must not lift it
from the paper.

Many children in Japan go to writing classes after school.

When artists paint pictures they can change things
as they go along but when I paint letters
I have to make special brush movements without stopping.
I cannot change anything, so the shapes
have to be exactly right first time.

I'm called Eri.
I am a model.

About five years ago I was shopping in Tokyo when I was
spotted by a man from a modeling agency.
He said he thought I'd make a good model and
that's how I got my first job.
I was photographed for the front cover of a girls' magazine.
We have 43 magazines for girls in Japan and
they all have sections on fashion and show business.
It was the first time that I'd ever been photographed
in a studio and I can still remember how nervous I was.

There are two kinds of modeling work in Japan.
One is fashion modeling, which is mainly for shows
and magazines.
The other is working for television commercials
and advertisements.
That's the kind I do all the time.

I work long hours and
often have to buy
a quick snack for lunch.

Today I am modeling
some new clothes for
holidays and weekends.
We came down to the
harbor for the photos
so that we could get
boats in the background.

I'm Michitada and I am a politician.

Japan's parliament is called the National Diet.
It has two sections, the House of Representatives and
the House of Councillors.
I am a member of the House of Councillors and
I belong to the Japanese Socialist Party.

Today I am speaking
in an important debate
in the House of Councillors.
I believe that we should
get rid of nuclear weapons
and I often speak about that
in our debates.

Every morning I get up at 7:30 a.m., read the newspapers
and watch the news on television.
I often attend a meeting after breakfast
before going to the House at 10:30 a.m.
There are more meetings in the evening and sometimes
they don't end until midnight.
The Diet is closed at weekends so I can go home, but
I don't get much rest because that's when I meet
the people who voted for me, and I try to solve their problems.

This is the National Diet building.
▼

My name is Mikio. I'm an engineer.

You may have heard of Sony videos, tape recorders, TVs and stereos.
I work as a design engineer for the Sony company in Tokyo.
One of my jobs was to design parts for our "Walkman" personal stereos, which we now sell to 170 countries.

◀ This is my drawing board in the design department at Sony Sound Ltd.

50

These are some of the
tape recorders and stereos
which have made Sony famous
all over the world.

Sony began in 1946 with only twenty workers.
Now it is a huge company with factories in the U.S.A.,
England, West Germany and many other countries.
We now have over 20,000 workers in the company!

My hobby is playing with old-fashioned tape recorders.
I love recording music on them and then editing the tapes.
At home I have a room set up like a recording studio and
I've recorded music on 800 reels of tape.

I am Toshio and I'm a fisherman.

You are never far from the sea in Japan, so fishing
has always been important to our way of life.
I fish in the Sagami Bay, south of Tokyo.
Most of my fish are sold to the people who live in the capital.
The Japanese enjoy seafood more than anything else.

This is where I moor
my fishing boat in the
harbor at Sagami Bay.
I set sail at 4:00 a.m. and
start fishing at 4:30 a.m.
every morning.

These fish are being sorted for the morning market.

We put out our nets in a box-shaped pattern to catch the fish.
It takes about an hour to pull in the nets again and then
we go back to the harbor to sort out the catch.
We get our fish ready for the fish auctions at about 7:00 a.m.
After the auction I can get back home for breakfast and begin
a day's work in the office!
I employ 15 people in my fishing company and there is always
lots of paperwork to do, as well as fishing.

I am Manjiro.
I'm an actor.

I act in *kabuki,* a kind of drama
which has been acted in Japan for hundreds of years.
Stories are acted out on stage with special words and
movements.
The actors wear the most beautiful kimonos and
a special kind of white makeup.
All the actors are men and the thinnest men act women's parts!
My father was a *kabuki* actor and I was only five years old
when I first went on stage.

Here I am in a scene from a *kabuki* story.
I have played many different parts but I always try
to become the character I am acting.

It takes me about 15 minutes to put on my makeup.

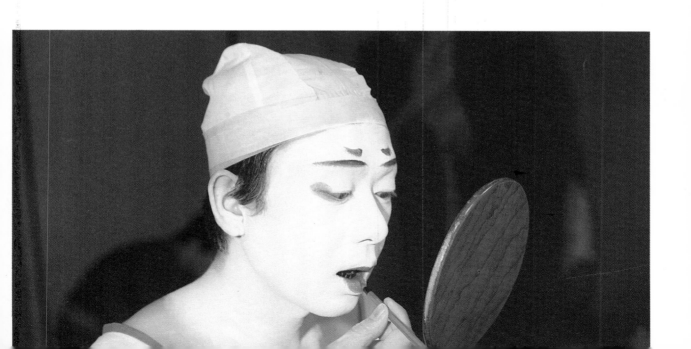

I am Hisayo.
I'm a teacher.

I have been an elementary school teacher for three years in the coastal town of Hiratsuki, south of Tokyo.

Japanese children have to work hard in school but that doesn't mean that then can't enjoy themselves!

I have a class of 7-year-olds and I teach them Japanese,
math, history, geology, science, art and physical education.
We also teach *yutori* which is about hobbies.
During *yutori* lessons the children play games,
look after animals, grow plants and play music.
I think teaching young children is interesting and enjoyable,
but it is also very hard work.

We eat our lunch in the classroom and the children
bring their own table napkins from home.
I sit with a different group each day so that
I can get to know them better.

Facts

Capital City The capital city of Japan is Tokyo.

Language People in Japan speak Japanese.

Money Japanese people pay for things with yen.
There are about 260 yen in $1.

Religion Most people in Japan are Buddhists.

People There are approximately 120,000,000 people
living in Japan.
Three-fourths of them live in cities.
The biggest cities are Tokyo, Osaka, Nagoya
and Kitakyushu.
Japan is one of the most
crowded countries in the world.

Weather Japan gets a lot of rain.
In summer it is warm and damp and
in winter it is mild and sunny.
The north of Japan can have
heavy falls of snow.
The best weather is in spring and fall,
when it is warm and sunny.

Government	Japan has an Emperor. The parliament is called the Diet. It has two houses, the House of Representatives and the House of Councillors.
Schools	Children from 3 to 6 years go to nursery school. From 6 to 12 years they go to elementary school, from 12 to 15 years to middle school and from 15 to 18 years to high school. Universities teach four-year degree courses.
Houses	There are enough houses for everyone but in the cities they are usually small and very expensive.
Farms	There are many mountains in Japan so only one-sixth of the land is used for farming. Farmers grow tobacco, tea, potatoes, rice, and wheat
Factories	Japanese factories make automobiles, electrical goods, metals, machines, chemicals, cement, pottery, cloth, glass, rubber, paper, oil, and ships.
News	Japan has an excellent radio and TV service. The NHK, or Japanese Broadcasting Corporation, has about 800 radio stations and 6,000 TV stations. There are 126 daily newspapers.